JOURNEY TO WHOLENESS

JOCELYN DESIREE

JOURNEY TO WHOLENESS
Jocelyn Desiree

Pecan Tree Publishing
www.pecantreebooks.com

New Voices | New Styles | New Vision –
Creating a New Legacy of Dynamic Authors and
Titles
Hollywood, FL

CONTENTS

INTRODUCTION

**"Trauma: a deeply distressing
or disturbing experience."**

- Oxford Languages, 2022

Life grants us many different experiences; many we could do without. Experiences that leave us hurt, confused, disgruntled, broken, and traumatized. Experiences like the loss of a loved one, divorce or a bad breakup, infidelity, abuse (physical, verbal, mental and/or emotional). If you can identify with any of these things, then God has sent me to you. Not just to show you that you are not alone, but for you to know that there is healing, there is breakthrough, there is restoration and there is VICTORY on the other side. I know you've heard it all before, but I want to be real and transparent as we walk through this journey together. I cannot promise that it's going to be easy, because change never is, but I can say that if you are willing to do the work, then you'll find yourself right where God wants you to be. I carried one of my favorite scriptures with me on my journey to wholeness, and I would love for you to keep close.

> "Don't be afraid, for I am with you. Don't be discouraged, for I am your God. I will strengthen you and help you. I will hold you up with my victorious right hand."
>
> *- Isaiah 41:10 (NLT)*

This passage encouraged me to not quit, but to keep going until God got me through to the other side of what I HAD to face. Yes, there will be moments of fear, doubt and frustration, but you must remember to stay focused on Him and keep going because He has you. He won't leave you nor forsake (emotionally abandon) you. I encourage you to stay committed to the journey because the promising contradiction of being broken - is becoming WHOLE.

Let's Go!

The Beginning

*"Yea though I walk through the val-
ley of the shadows of death, I will
fear no evil…"*

- Psalms 23:4 (NLT)

I, Jocelyn Desiree am a divorcee, but I am not the product of divorce. I was raised in a Christian based household by two loving parents. Parents who have been married now for over 30 plus years. So, it's safe to say that being a divorcee did not come from the lack of having an example of what a healthy, loving marriage looked like. I am not what society would label a stereotypical divorcee based on family history. So, where did I go wrong?

Since high school, I desired to experience the kind of love I saw at home. The attributes of their love has always been so inspiring. Growing up, I experienced a marital relationship through them that was supportive, nurturing, wholesome, and progressive. After several decades of marriage, my parents move as a well-orchestrated team. They make each other a priority and ensure that God is the center of EVERYTHING they do. And though we know that no relationship is perfect, I desired a love like theirs. First Corinthians 13:4-7 (NLT) states, "Love is patient and kind. Love is not jealous, boastful, proud, or rude. It does not demand its own way. It is not irritable, and it keeps no record of being wronged. It does not rejoice about injustice but rejoices whenever the truth wins out. Love never gives up, never loses faith, is always hopeful, and endures through every circumstance." That's what I was desperate for. I needed to find someone to love and someone that was willing to love me and support me in the same manner. Sadly, I fell short.

From the time that I was able to exclusively date (in my teenage years), I experienced a lot of heartbreak. Mostly from rejection, or guys only wanting me for sex, and this took a toll on me. I grew tired of jumping from relationship to relationship and my desire to be with someone who was willing to choose me, love all of me and value the woman he'd have in me increased. At the age of 20, I thought I found that. We were so compatible on paper. You know as ladies we tend to create a list of the type of husband WE want. My list, which I created at 19, was a culmination of the good things from all of my past relationships. I jotted down all of the qualities I liked in my ex-boyfriends and wouldn't mind having again; and then I thought about what I wished was different, and I wrote those down too. Well, who I found allowed me to check off everything on my list of good qualities. He was tall and handsome, he came from a two-parent home, he attended church regularly, he had a job, no kids, we had good conversations, but most importantly we were friends first. One thing that I wasn't willing or ready to admit to myself at the time was that I didn't know myself yet. I was still in a place of trying to figure out who I was and what I had to offer as a woman. I should've taken my time; but I didn't. I found myself being anxious and flat out desperate. We exchanged the words, "I love you" in the first month or so of dating. We all know telling someone that you love them takes things to a greater and deeper level. I was so caught up in my feelings because I was determined that he was going to be the one. I had failed so many times relationally, that I needed to prove to myself that I could have a strong, lasting relationship. However, I should've stopped and asked God what He wanted for me. Instead, I imposed on God what I wanted for myself. I never stopped to acknowledge that I was out of order.

I already didn't know how much work marriage was, but I especially didn't know how much more difficult it was going to be OUTSIDE of the will of God. What do I mean?

Because I didn't acknowledge how God wanted me to do things or move in His timing, my new life started out very rocky. We got engaged and had a plan to wait for at least a year before we got married. BUT I got pregnant. Yes, little miss church girl got pregnant; not because I didn't have standards and values, but because I chose not to follow them. I chose to relax everything I was taught because I felt that if I was going to keep this man, I was going to have to please him by any means necessary. Plus, I loved him, so, no harm no foul, right?

Even before we got engaged, I was already SO pressed to be married. I wanted it so bad and now, with me expecting, I wanted it even more! As a man, he wasn't too concerned about having a wedding. I, on the other hand, had already been planning a wedding. I had a dress picked out, I'd chosen my bridesmaids and I had a wedding planner. Of course, we were going to get married in a church with all of our loved ones. It was going to be grand. Yet I threw all of it out the window and flushed the money down the drain. Crazy right? Yes,

I compromised and sacrificed the wedding I had dreamed about just to rush and get married. And though some may think that he pressured me to do this, he didn't. He didn't have to. You see, before I found out I was pregnant, we had a what if conversation. If I ended up pregnant, what would I do. I said that I wouldn't mind getting married sooner or just going to the courthouse. Well, when the what if became a reality, he held me to my word. I hated giving up the wedding that every girl dreams of, but the pressure of raising a child weighed more on me. I convinced myself that allocating the wedding money to parenthood was much more important. And, I didn't want to have a baby out of wedlock; plus, I was afraid that I was going to lose the man I loved if I didn't make a decision. So, I went to the courthouse and said, "I do".

I know you may be wondering where my parents were in all of this and how they felt. Well, they had been there praying for me and trying to give my hard-headed self the best guidance they could, but because I thought I was grown and I knew it all, I didn't listen.

"Just wait, Jocelyn" they said. "What's your rush?" they asked. This seemed like major disapproval to me and fighting with them was not something I was willing to face. My thought was, it is better to just do it and smooth it over with them later. So, on the afternoon of August 24, 2009, I got married. There was no family, no friends, no support. Honestly, the entire day felt wrong. I remember standing under the little arch in the courthouse and I looked over at the empty chairs and my heart sank because I missed my family. Everything within me knew that it wasn't supposed to go this way, but the decision was made and there was no turning back.

Two days after we said I do, yes, two days later, I broke the news of my wifely status to my mom. I was strategic, making sure that I did it over the phone, while she was at work, and not face-to-face because I was terrified of her reaction. I mean can you blame me? Months prior, I had to tell my parents, who are pastors, that I had gotten pregnant and now I had gone behind their backs, to the courthouse and gotten married. That was one of the shortest, most intense conversations (if I can even call it that) that my mother and I have ever had. I said, "I wanted to let you know that I just left the courthouse. We decided to go ahead and get married." Her response was simply, "Bye Jocelyn." She hung up the phone. I knew she was FURIOUS. One of my biggest regrets was compromising what I wanted in a dream wedding but more than that, getting married without my family being there to celebrate with me. That hurt my mom to her core, and I couldn't take it back. Instead, I defended the decision by saying that it was my choice.

Throughout the first years of my marriage, the relationship between myself and my family became very strained. I barely saw them and in hindsight, that was my fault. I was so busy trying to please my husband that I forfeited what truly mattered to me. I got pregnant the summer before my second year of college, so I told myself that I would take a break and go back after the baby was born, but I never did. So now there was no wedding and no degree, just me, this baby and the man that checked off everything on my immature relationship list. By this time there was tension between all parties involved and I was in the middle. My parents wanted more for my life and were extremely disappointed, but I decided to make my whole life about him. Everything was what he wanted, from the church we attended, to the city we lived in. I was being more than a submissive wife, I became, what I'd call, the accommodating wife. I thought submitting was doing what pleased my husband because he was the head of our family. I didn't understand that submission did not mean being manipulated. And manipulation was prevalent in our relationship, but I didn't recognize it. He wasn't willing to leave the church that his parents pastored, so he convinced me to leave my church. He said that was submission. Manipulation with him always came with a scripture. He wasn't willing to live with my family while we worked to find and afford our own place because of the tension between us. So, we moved in with his parents. It wasn't about my comfort as the pregnant wife, it was about his comfort and needs. There was even a time before this transition that I considered staying with my parents until I had the baby, but he was not having it. While I was at my parent's house one day, before our wedding, the idea of me staying with my parents until the baby comes was on his mind, he came to take my engagement ring. He felt I was choosing my family over being with him. That shook me and triggered the fear of losing love again, so I left home and moved with him. Before I knew it, I was isolated from my friends and isolated from my family. All I had was him, his family, and our daughter.

Be careful what you ask for because you just might get it. I didn't know what I was asking for when I begged God to be married. I learned the literal meaning of, "knock and the door shall be opened unto you"- Matthew 7:8 (NLT). It was like God said, "Okay Jocelyn, you think your way is right? You think this is what you want? Do you want to choose to please him instead of me? Well, let me show you the cost."

CHAPTER TWO

The Breakdown

The thing about being broken is that it seems as though everything around you is falling apart. Nothing ever seems to go as planned, good days are few and far in-between, there is never a bright side to anything and finding something to smile about - well you get the point and that was me.

Being young and not yet having anything to call our own was hard. Adjusting to being married was hard. Dating someone and living and being in the same space with them are TOTALLY different things. I was now in this man's space and a part of his world. Within the first year of marriage, I started seeing him for who he really was. Red Flag: He didn't listen to anybody except his mama! Red Flag: He has a major attitude problem. Red Flag: He tends to speak recklessly. Our first argument, he cursed me out and disrespected me to shame. I remember I packed a bag for myself and the baby, but he wouldn't let me take her. I left and went to my parents' house. He called and called and called. I subscribed to only having the responsibility of letting him know where I was and that I was safe, but I didn't want to talk. I was so upset and left so quickly that I took all of our daughter's milk so he couldn't feed her. With that, he drove 30 minutes to where I was not for his wife or his marriage, but to bring me the baby....RED FLAG!

In February of 2011 we finally were able to move into our own apartment. It wasn't much, but it was ours. We were still having ups and downs, but I thought it was normal in a fresh marriage. I remember the day I looked at myself in the mirror and didn't recognize who I was anymore. I was once bold, confident, and resilient; someone who was never afraid to speak her mind or do whatever I needed or wanted to do for me. I became insecure, angry, depressed, and full of regret. I remember the day like it was yesterday. My husband and I had gotten into an argument about what I cooked for dinner. It was the argument that made me fully aware of how toxic my marriage was and the direction my marriage was going. The day I realized that nothing ever seemed good enough for him, not even me. It was like he never found satisfaction in anything I brought to the table. So, this one evening before church, he cursed me over a pan of Shepherd's Pie. Yes, you read it right, a pan of Shepherd's Pie! I was called all sorts of names and minimized as a wife, a mother, and a woman, because he felt I didn't make enough food. This was not the first time or the only thing that he would come down hard on me about, and it also wasn't the first time I snapped. By this time, we were about two years in, and now parents of two beautiful baby girls who weren't strangers to our many, MANY spats. Still, I would try to not lose it in front of them. So, I stormed into the bathroom of our apartment, screaming, fuming, like I wanted to explode. I had energy I needed to exert, and I needed to do it fast, so I started swinging. Next thing I knew, there were two huge holes in the back of the bathroom door.

Once I calmed down, I burst into tears. One, because I couldn't believe I had enough anger in me to punch holes into a door. Two, I cried because this wasn't me. I hated who I was becoming. Always on the defense, always on guard, crying more than I smiled, compromising my standards and my values, allowing someone to easily affect my character and behavior in a negative way. I had lost myself to a man who said he loved me but treated me like crap and made me feel worthless. There were so many other arguments. Some big and some small, but no matter the magnitude, they would always last for days, sometimes weeks. We could argue about something as simple as the girls getting their hair done or spending the night with my parents and it would turn into huge blow-ups and cause more division between us.

I saw something change in my husband after the day that he decided to have a private conversation with his parents about how we would no longer attend their church. We both agreed to this decision because we were hungry for more spiritually. That was the moment he felt as though he was put in the middle of having to choose between me and his mama. I know that his family was hurt and felt a bit abandoned because we played a significant role in their ministry. My then husband, had recently become a licensed minister and we both were leading the praise and worship team every Sunday. I know in that private conversation, there were some things said that I'm still not privy to, but I know that whatever was said caused immediate tension. It seemed I was to blame for pulling their son away, however, it was truly more of his decision than it was mine. He was head of the house. Needless to say, the more difficult his relationship became with his family, the more difficult he became toward me. It really took a toll on me mentally and emotionally. There were many days that I dreaded going home. I spent many days and nights on my bathroom floor screaming and crying in agony because of the verbal, mental and emotional abuse. I would drive to an empty parking lot around the corner from where we lived to escape the arguing and breathe and pray. It was in the moments that he would verbally bash me, intimidate me, and belittle me that I learned the saying, "Sticks and stones may break my bones, but words will never hurt me" was an ABSOLUTE LIE!

Why didn't I just leave? Well, mentally for me it wasn't that simple. I felt stuck, almost imprisoned. I remember saying to myself, "I'd rather die than live another day like this." I didn't know how to move though. I was isolated from my family, who I distanced myself from. They had no clue what was happening behind closed doors with us. No one did. I felt responsible for the situation I was in. I prayed and wanted so bad to be married and this is what I got. Why couldn't God just fix it, is what I often wondered and prayed. I would ask myself countless times out of guilt and shame, "Jocelyn, what did you do?" I loved my children but hated that I brought them into such toxicity, and it was my responsibility to get them out. I knew that I had to figure something out when my oldest daughter came to give me advice in the middle of an argument, I was having with her dad. She had grown so accustomed to our behavior that one day she, suggested that I not fight back. So, in this moment, she walked up to me at the age of three or four and whispered in my ear, "Mommy, remember what I said." I immediately calmed down. It was as if God himself was using her to show me that not only did my girls see it, but they understood what was happening around them and it had become their norm.

While on this rollercoaster of my marriage, I began, after four and a half years, praying for God to realign me with the purpose and plan He had for my life. The word of God says that God ordains for us to live a life of peace, but peace was the furthest thing from me. I questioned, how I could minister every Sunday as a vessel that God would use, and my life be such a mess. I felt as though I was living a lie. I needed God to either make things better in my marriage, rescue me or grant me a way of escape.

I was home one day and of course we were arguing -AGAIN. I was growing so tired of it because I'm not a combative person, plus I just wanted to love the man, not go to war with him. So once again, I escaped the arguing, grabbed the keys, jumped in the car, and went to my empty parking lot. My prayers had intensified. Why? Because I was at war, I realized, this was more spiritual than natural. We are spiritual beings living a natural experience and what we naturally see as characteristics of a person can be translated spiritually as the spirit a person can possess and/or operate in. The spirit of Jezebel is one that portrays the characteristics of manipulation and control; that was the spirit that was becoming more and more dominant in my home. I had to learn the art of spiritual warfare. I had to learn how to pray and command order, peace, and unity in my home. I began to ask God to show me how to exist in my marriage and to guide me on how I should move forward. So, in my empty parking lot, I prayed, I warred, I cried, I screamed, but I recall a specific prayer that I believe changed things for me.

I said, "God, I want you to fix everything that's wrong in my marriage, but if this man cannot line up with the purpose and the plans that you have set for my life and go the way that you ordain for us to go, then he's got to go."

I've always had a heart to go, do, and be whatever God wanted, but I knew in the marriage I chose, I had messed up and it was time to make it right. I learned the hard way that being out of the will of God is a dangerous place to be. I felt it in every way. Everything in life seemed hard. We never seemed to ever have enough financially, I was often sick, my kids were often sick, and we could never seem to get ahead or get along. I wanted to live in the favor of God, in the love of God, but most of all in the peace of God. So, a few months after praying this prayer, God granted me some instructions. This was during a season that we were displaced in ministry and having a church home. However, God granted me instructions to have a conversation with my then husband. He gave me the words to say to explain how we should attend my parent's church (my original home church) until God showed us something different.

I realized after about five years into my marriage that I had compromised my relationship with family and friends. I compromised what I desired for my life. I compromised ME. I remember my mom telling me, "Jocelyn, there is a difference between being submissive and being subjective." I believe that as a wife being submissive means to truly honor your husband, to respect your husband and be the HELP MEET or helper that God has created us to be. I LEARNED that it's NOT doing everything he says and agreeing to move forward with everything he wants to do. And it is DEFINITELY not being his COVER UP for every unwise decision that he chooses to make. That is being CONTROLLED! Being MANIPULATED! Being SUBJECT to a person and what THEY want your life to look like.

Now that I think about it, if I consider all the characteristics of how I was treated, from being controlled, isolated, manipulated, verbally abused, mentally and emotionally abused, and made to feel like a piece of meat; I think it's safe to say frankly, that I was his whore, and he was my john. You may think that that's an exaggeration, but this man would walk around for days, in the same house with me, and not utter a word to me or the only conversation he had for me was harsh criticism. He looked at me with disgust and nothing I did was ever good enough, including not having sex with him whenever he felt like it. He would often make me feel guilty, by throwing scriptures at me. He would rant about how I'm supposed to be "the savior of his body", but if you read Ephesians 5:23 (KJV) it clearly states, "For the husband is the head of the wife, even as Christ is the head of the church: and he is the saviour of the body." So, what about me? What about what he was doing to my body, my mind, my spirit, and my heart? I was at one of the lowest places I had ever been in my life, and nobody knew until….

It was a Saturday in September of 2015. By this time, we had been married for 6 years and things had gotten so strained with us, that I removed myself from our bedroom and started sleeping on the couch. We weren't speaking or having any interaction with one another and the tension in our house was so thick, you could cut it with a chainsaw. By this time things in our marriage and our home had taken a hard left. It happened when his family caught wind that we were attending my parents church. Part of me thinks that they felt betrayed in some way. He was feeling the heat from his family.

That Saturday, I decided to get out of the house. No destination in mind, I just wanted to go. I got up to get the only key that we had to OUR SUV, but it wasn't on the hook. Where was the key? He had it, tucked away somewhere so I had to ask for it in order to leave. Highly annoyed, I asked for the key and in a truly controlling fashion he pressed me about where I was going, but because I didn't have a destination, leaving was a problem. We argued because he accused me of lying and going to see someone, Finally, he relinquished the key. I turned to walk out of the bedroom then suddenly felt something hit me in the back of my head. I turned and looked down to see what it was. It was an ink pen. Now as small as it was, it was something about the fact that he would actually throw and object at me to hit me that changed something in me. It was as if my light bulb finally lit up. I didn't get angry or lash out. I didn't pick up something else to hit him back. It was as if the Holy Spirit took over - literally. As much as this situation warranted a harsh reaction, instead I was shockingly very calm.

I turned and picked up the ink pen, walked over to where he was laying on the bed with an attitude as if he were untouchable. I sat on the bed next to him, looked him in his face, and with a confident yet calm tone I said, "I'm done." I could tell that those two words took him by surprise because he wanted me to clarify what I was done with. Once I made it clear that I was done with him, he snapped. I had never seen such rage in his eyes as he towered over me on the bed, yelling and screaming in my face that I could leave but I wasn't taking HIS car. That was the first time I felt that type of fear. Though he showed restraint by not hitting me, the aggression, the hostility, the rage assured me that his behavior was now becoming unpredictable.

Then I did something, that I should've done long before. I called my mom. I could barely talk through my crying and being so shaken. I could only manage to get out the words, "Please come get me, please!" While I waited, I made sure to stay away from him, so an already intense situation did not escalate. Within minutes, his family was knocking at our door. I did not know that my parents called his parents. Soon after they arrived, my parents did as well. Everyone was concerned and of course we both had different versions. He said I was overreacting. He completely missed the fact that I was at my wit's end. Thankfully, my girls were unaware of the severity of the day and the moment. Plus, they were so used to friction that it was just another incident for them. Our families on the other hand were taken aback that things were that rough between us; but it was what it was, and I was tired of hiding it. I needed help.

I packed a duffle bag for myself and my girls, and we left. I felt safe back at home with my family. And when I say safe, I mean mentally, spiritually, emotionally, and physically, which was more than I could say about the space I shared with him. There was no judgment, no deep conversations about the occurrences that transpired that day. They just allowed me the space to breathe and gather my thoughts. After a couple of days, I sat with my mom, and she simply asked me if I was okay and how I wanted to move forward. I honestly didn't know. All I knew was that I wanted peace. I didn't want to make a rash, emotional decision.

There was however a decision I needed to face, not just for myself, but for my children. Whatever decision I made I was going to have to live with it. My mom said something to me as we talked that sticks with me to this day. She first asked, "Have you done everything on your part to make it work?" I said, "Probably not." So, she gave me this wisdom, "Do everything you know to do to make it work so that if you choose to leave, you won't have any regrets." With that said, after a week apart, I went back. I went back with boundaries and non-negotiables. We decided to seek professional counseling to work through our issues as I went back to my spot on the couch, sleeping with a knife under my pillow. Crazy right?!

For the next three weeks, there was nothing but arguing, fussing, and fighting. Fights about the kids, fights about money, fights about work, and fights about our families. But to me one of the biggest fights was about church. Once his family found out about the church arrangement, he stopped attending church with me and became very secretive about if or what church he was giving his bi-weekly contributions or what we call our tithes to. Now let me explain one thing about me and how I was raised. I am and will ALWAYS be a faithful tithes payer and being cursed with a curse is not on my agenda.

Malachi 3:9-10 (NLT) states, "You are under a curse for your whole nation has been cheating me. Bring all the tithes into the storehouse so there will be enough food in my Temple. If you do," says the Lord of Heaven's Armies, "I will open up the windows of heaven for you. I will pour you out a blessing so great you won't have enough room to take it in! Try it! Put me to the test!"

The lack of transparency in this area motivated me to stop the direct deposit of my payroll from going into our joint account and open a separate independent bank account. Our house was now divided, in another area. From sleeping separately, separate bank accounts, and even who was going to pay what bill. It was the most toxic cycle of foolishness I had ever experienced, but when I finally got tired of fighting and losing, I decided to leave again; and stick to it. The straw that broke the camel's back was on a night in October, only a month after being back in the same space with him. We were having a conversation, after our daughters had been put to bed, about getting another car because operating with one vehicle wasn't going to continue to work. I didn't mention it, but something about it just made me feel like I was being held hostage and it was a form of control. You see, my parent's offered to match the dollar amount of whatever we saved for a vehicle down payment. Something about the offer threatened him and began to spew obscene insults about my parents and our relationship. He even said that my father was my "man on the side" who I preferred to take care of me. I had an epiphany. Things weren't going to change. He wasn't going to change. No matter what I did, no matter my approach, this wasn't going to work.

Sometimes as women we like to say that we know our worth and what we deserve but will never admit how stupid we get when we're in love. The craziness we will endure or the abuse we accept. And we do this all just to say that we have a man. Too scared to leave because of the embarrassment that may come, the questions we'd have to answer, and the explanations that we'd have to give. But when you truly get sick and tired, when your tired is tired and you're at your lowest, at your breaking point, none of the repercussions that you may have to face even matter. Freedom becomes a priority.

I remember the evening that I told him that I had had enough. I had reached my place of no regrets and no return. He asked me if I still loved him. He even asked if I was going to put him on child support. Truth of the matter was that I was no longer in love with him, and I had no intention on keeping him from his children and I made sure to be honest and transparent about that. Too much damage had been done, too much hurt had been caused and all I wanted was to be free of the tormenting pain that had become my norm.

Before it was all said and done, he had taken the car key, and my house key. He took the girls and I to work and to school the next morning as he usually did. Later that morning I put my plan of escape in place. My parents were going to get my children from school, my dad was going to allow me to borrow his truck so that after I left work I could go back to the apartment and get my belongings. However, my now estranged husband told me that I couldn't get back into our apartment to retrieve my belongings until I gave him back HIS ring (the ring I helped pay for). Needless to say, I let him have it. I even agreed to continue going to counseling because I wanted a change in my marriage more than I wanted a divorce. I left the car, the apartment and gave him back the ring in exchange for my freedom. I left with $300 to my name and unable to find my luggage, I had to pack two garbage bags with clothes for me and the girls. Everything else was sacrificed for the sake of peace. And where it could've been a fight for a lot of the stuff I left behind, it wasn't worth it, because that's all it was -STUFF. I remember walking back into my parents' house the night that I left him, and my mom was standing at the front door with her arms stretched out to embrace me, letting me know that it was okay if I wanted to fall apart. I hugged her and I said, "I'm okay. I don't have time to fall apart. I have kids to take care of."

You see, I had one goal in mind, one destination, one objective and that was to get to a place of PEACE. So, if that meant leaving my home, giving up my car, losing furniture, jewelry, or leaving behind some clothes and shoes that I couldn't carry, then so be it. Those THINGS could be replaced, but I had lost stuff of greater value that I couldn't afford to lose anymore of. Time was wasted and I forfeited the vision I had for my life. I lost myself. I lost sight of who I was, what I wanted and what I deserved. I allowed a man to matter more and put him above anything and everybody, including God. But I am truly thankful that God granted me His mercy and His faithfulness and saw me through until He led me out.

I'm thankful even now for all the support and wisdom God sent my way that helped me to get out. He gave me angels to give me just what I needed, when and how I needed it. Someone was always there as a resource, an advisor, a bodyguard, a shoulder to lean on, etc. But I also know that if God wouldn't have given me the courage and granted me the way of escape, I wouldn't have done it. Not on my own strength because I didn't have any. Not on my own intellect because I couldn't see a way out through all the tears, anger, and frustration. It taught me that when God presents an opportunity, to not hesitate to take advantage of it. Often times we continuously battle back and forth within ourselves about what we should do, when God has already made the pathway plain and the answer clear.

So, I moved back in with my parents, who always made it clear that I always had a place to come back to. Thank God! I didn't have much but I had everything I needed. I was still attending church with my parents because that's where God planted me. I took my time and didn't jump right back into ministry because I needed the time to be poured into. I was hurting, I was embarrassed, and I was broken. Getting to that place of peace was becoming even harder because a new fight was on the rise....DIVORCE.

Yes, the "D" word. For six months it was separation. The period of time where I prayed, pondered, and sought out my next steps. The time where love and loyalty were tested. In this time the professional counseling that we were getting was a bust. She chose a side instead of helping us to sift through our many issues and working toward a place of healing and reconciliation. That was when I knew that we were going to need God's help to fix what we had going on.

In December of 2016 I was at a Sunday church service during our Ladies Conference and a prophetess was praying for me and speaking over my life. And I'll never forget what she told me God was saying. She prophesied to me, and I quote, "Jocelyn, the Lord said that if you decide to leave, He will cover you and if you decide to stay, He'll cover you." I was rattled! The truth of the matter is that I didn't want the responsibility of making that decision. I was so afraid of making the wrong choice because I felt like I had made so many bad choices thus far. I went right back to God and said, "Lord, that responsibility is too great. I can't make that decision because I don't know what's right for me. You know my ending before my beginning and God, you know who I'm dealing with. I just need you to lead me and guide me. Make the decision for me that will put me where You will have for me to be. Where I will have peace and I can be happy."

This man would not let me rest. The battles had become even harder and more intense. After countless fights, threats and the police being called, my back was suddenly up against the wall. In one incident, my boss had to call the police after he caused such a scene on my job on the previous day. He attempted to pick up our daughter, but because his hostility had intensified, she wasn't comfortable leaving with him. She kicked, hollered, and screamed as he carried her to the car. Anybody who didn't know that he was her father would've thought she was being kidnapped. It was such a heart-wrenching thing to watch, but I couldn't refuse him the right to pick her up. After a few minutes of him battling with her, he allowed her to stay with me. At the time of the incident, my boss wasn't at work, but when she caught wind of what took place, calling the police was at the top of her list of things to do the next morning. I'll never forget the conversation I had with the officer. He explained that as a father he has rights and even if our daughter(s) doesn't want to go, they would have to allow him the right to her. My thought process shifted from protecting me, to protecting my children. I wasn't willing to play tug-a-war over my children and put them in the middle of a fight that had the potential to get uglier. The officer suggested that the only way I could protect them and protect myself was to get a custody timesharing agreement, which was only going to come with filing for divorce. So, for the safety and stability of my children, I called a divorce attorney, and after a $2500 retainer fee and signing documents, the paperwork was filed.

The next six months of going through the divorce process was extremely exhausting. If you've ever been through a divorce, you know that it's comparable to a death. You find yourself going through a grieving process (and we all grieve in diverse ways). Problem was, I had to realize that I wasn't the only one grieving.

He was grieving and our children were grieving as well.

The separation honestly didn't hit me immediately or soon after. I was processing it in anger for so long that by the time the hurt actually hit me, months had passed. But when it hit, it hit me hard. I spent an entire night crying and screaming in anguish because the hurt ran so deep. The next day I couldn't eat, I couldn't think; I could barely function. It was like something in me had died and I knew it wasn't coming back.

My oldest daughter was a daddy's girl, but our separation became the turning point in their relationship. My youngest didn't quite understand the severity of the situation, but she felt it. She knew something was wrong and she didn't like the feeling or the idea that our family was no longer together. As a mother, it broke my heart and I felt guilty because I knew that it was only going to become more difficult. Why did I say that? Because of how he was grieving. His grief was spiteful and vindictive. His grief sought out attention in the worse kind of ways. His grief caused him to lash out on our kids when he was really upset with me. His grief caused him to unnecessarily pull our children in the middle of our separation by telling them that I was trying to take them away from him, which was far from the truth. His grief caused him to attack me and my family on every popular social media platform.

Hurt people, hurt people. And where I wanted to take the time to peacefully process how one major chapter of my life was ending and another was beginning, he wouldn't let me. I thought by leaving, it would change his behavior toward me. Make him see my value and my worth as a woman, a wife, and a mother. But, No! It taught me that no matter how much you want someone to change, their change has to be their choice. No matter how much I prayed, he was going to be who he chose to be.

At this point I wasn't sure who this person was that I was dealing with, and it was quite scary. I found myself wondering how I could've missed this. Was he always like this? Was what or who I fell in love with even real?

One thing I was sure about over anything else, was that it was toxic.

As hard as the decision was for me to walk away for good, it gave me a new strength. However, it was still a fight for me to free myself from the hold he had on me. If you've ever been in an abusive relationship, whether physical, verbal, mental or emotional, you can relate to the sense of control and fear that that person places over you. He knew the exact buttons to press that would affect me mentally and emotionally. His manipulation skills were impeccable. He knew just what to say and how to play on my emotions to get what he wanted out of me. I had to realize quickly that it wasn't him that needed to change it was me.

I had to learn to stop reacting when he would press my buttons, until I eventually got to the place of hiding my buttons. I had to learn to silence myself when he would try to pick an argument with me or attack me verbally. This man wasn't just in my head, he was tied to my soul and as much as I was free physically, I was still being held hostage mentally and emotionally. So, breaking free was going to be on me. It was a long and hard fight, but because I was determined to get to a place of COMPLETE peace, I was willing to fight for my life. I had to realize that fighting and going back and forth with words and triggering behaviors was easy, but it wasn't what was required to obtain the victory I was looking for. I needed a different type of strategy. You see when you know exactly what you're up against, you don't go in blind. You stop to understand your opponent so that you can build an effective and productive strategy. During this process, I had some epic fails. Times where he would insult me, threaten to pop up on me, or tell lies concerning me and my children to intimidate me. In those moments I would allow my emotions to get the best of me by responding in irrational ways. I had to remember, just as I knew him, he knew me too. He knew my triggers and he never hesitated to use them against me.

I learned to turn my epic fails into lessons learned so that I could progress in what was an uphill battle. The insults about my parenting or me as a person were hard hits. The lies he told about me and even to me as if I didn't live the truth, were hard hits. His toying with my kids' emotions was hard. But I took the hits with grace. I responded when a response was necessary, and I was silent when a response wasn't warranted. I did my best to maintain my self-control because I kept in the forefront of my mind that my children were always watching and always listening, and I was their example of how to handle things.

The thing about being broken is that, in most cases, it's the person or people that's closest to us that breaks us. The ones that take up the most space in our hearts. We never expect THOSE people to be the ones who cause us the most pain or create our deepest wounds. I still don't have the answer as to how someone who says they love me could treat me the way my ex-husband did, but he did. He broke me, but I came to realize that the breaking was necessary. If I were never broken, God wouldn't have had the opportunity to put me back together and make me new. I know it sounds cliché, but when I say that God made me new, I mean He made my life BRAND NEW.

CHAPTER THREE

The Coming Out

After six excruciatingly long months the divorce was finalized. Being happily divorced, but broken is such an oxymoron, but that was me. The very day that my divorce was finalized on October 12, 2016, I felt like I could breathe again. Yet, I was still wounded and battling with unresolved issues. My prayer then became, "God, what do I do with these broken pieces? How do I move forward?" I was a blank slate, and I wasn't sure who I was as a grown and now single woman and mother. However, I felt as though God had given me another chance to get me together.

Some of us come out of one traumatic situation to jump right into another one. This is where and how we mess up - again. We use rebound people as distractions because we don't want to go through the process of healing, growing, and learning from the hurt, mistakes, and the breakdown of our past relationships. We don't take the time to hold ourselves accountable to see where we went wrong and how not to take that into our future relationships. We have grown so accustomed to being with someone, that we've developed a fear of being alone. But the truth of the matter is, how will you ever know who you are or what you have to offer to anyone if you don't take some time to get to know you. Every relationship is a lesson. Especially those that are long term. You learn what you want and don't want. What you like and what you can't tolerate. Mostly, what you deserve and how you deserve to be treated. It should also teach you how or in what areas you can be a better partner. It matures you if you allow it to.

However, in the breakdown of a relationship, we tend to always look at what the other person did wrong, place blame, walk away and then we're on to the next victim. But is there ever a period of self-reflection? Do we realize that when we don't take the time to truly heal, grow, or self-reflect that we are only setting the next person up to have a detrimental and/or traumatic experience with us? We look to them to be our cover up. The person we can hide our brokenness behind. They waste time getting to know the broken you, thinking that it's the real you. Or they want to fix you and help piece you back together not understanding that you and God are the only ones that can accomplish that task. Now you become the hurt person who's hurting people.

I didn't care for this to be my story. Mostly, I was afraid of making the same mistake twice. So, I did a lot of praying asking God to order my steps in this process of moving forward. I didn't want to be the bitter ex-wife or the bitter baby mama. I began to ask God to make me whole and show me what life could be after divorce. I didn't have closure, but I was in a place where I didn't care to wait for it either. I didn't care to wait for someone to give me permission to move on with my life and heal. I came to understand that my now ex-husband had his process, and I had mine. It seemed that he was fixated on me and making sure that I understood that he was hurting, and he wasn't ready to let me go. I, on the other hand, was focused on my mental and emotional well-being and the well-being of our children. I wanted to, I NEEDED to forgive him, and he made it hard because he was always doing something to attack me mentally or emotionally. His actions, would at times, set me back. But purifying my heart was most important for me. Let's be real, HE WASN'T GOING ANYWHERE. Yes, we were divorced, but we were still connected through our girls which meant that no matter what, I was going to have to deal with this man.

The first step was making sure that my children could adjust to our new way of living and being. They were being shuffled back and forth between myself and their father. Seeing and hearing both sides of a broken marriage and family. They were witnessing two hurt individuals trying to process this new life in two separate ways and it affected them gravely. As young as they were, they understood so much and expressed it as best as they could. They were caught in the crossfire of a battle that they had absolutely nothing to do with. I remember being in tears praying and asking God to help me help them. I had such mommy guilt and I wanted to fix the hurt I was causing them. So, the Lord instructed me to find a counselor for my daughters and me. Now, I had tried therapy through professional marriage counseling before so and it didn't go so well so, I was a little apprehensive, but the kids and I needed help. Now I am a firm believer of seeking wise counsel and we could have just gone to my parents to get counseling, seeing that they are the Pastor and First Lady, but in this case, they were my parents. There were a few variants that played a role in me going in a different direction. I trust them always as my spiritual leaders and when I needed them in that capacity, they were 1000% there for us. But as my natural leaders, all I really needed was their support. I felt as though I had done so much damage and brought so much drama to their lives already and the things I needed to discuss to move forward from concerning my marriage and concerning my children, would have only traumatized them, angered them, and made matters worse and more difficult to move on from. So, I sought out a family therapist.

I learned in my previous experience that finding a therapist can be a hit or miss. I'm mature enough to know that you can't allow just anybody to pour into you. Some people have the gift to nourish, encourage and motivate and then some people come to contaminate. I needed help being pushed in a new direction where I was going to experience progress, growth, and healing. I met this BEAUTIFUL soul who I noticed immediately was very patient and non-judgmental, but what I appreciated about her the most was that she always kept it real with me. Never pulled any punches. If I was the problem, if I was holding myself back in any way, if my perspective was wrong or my approach was a little too extra in certain situations, she always let me know constructively and with such grace. As I began going to see her, I didn't take my kids with me right away. I took the time to assess if she was the right fit for me first, and to debrief her on the saga that was my life. From our first meeting I felt so comfortable with her, as if I'd known her for years. This was a vibe that I never experienced with the marriage counselor. This therapist listened to me and allowed me to process the different things I was feeling and experiencing. Helping me to see what didn't make sense, because let's be honest my ex's manipulation had become such a norm that I had to now sit and pick apart the things that didn't make sense, so I'd know what truth was and what was a false sense of reality. Things like, his being overly obsessed with my whereabouts or the whereabouts of our children wasn't him being protective, it was him being controlling and that wasn't healthy. There were no tricks, no deep exercises, or trances. We talked like two good girlfriends.

Once my girls had the opportunity to meet her, they immediately fell in love with her just as I did. She was so warm and welcoming to them to the point where they just opened up and unloaded all of their feelings about this new place in our lives. Within the first few sessions, I began to see and understand how distraught and unhappy my children truly were. On one hand I was glad that they felt secure enough with me to openly share both their thoughts and feelings, both good and bad. However, the things I heard broke my heart.

Not only did the girls and I have this personal family counselor, but we were also assigned a co-parenting counselor to see separately. I know you're wondering who assigned the counselor. Well, right after our divorce was finalized, The Children's Father decided to call Child Protective Services (CPS) on me. He submitted a false claim that I had been abusing our girls. There was an investigation and there were no findings of abuse. Because both the divorce and the time sharing were fresh, it was the recommendation of CPS that both parties attend co-parenting counseling. I welcomed all the help I could get in making this new adjustment to co-parenting with someone I would have rather not had any dealings with at all, but I had no choice. Co-parenting counseling was a major help when it came to me learning how to not be driven by my emotions, stick to the facts and set boundaries.

While our family counselor helped me to sift through my emotions, the co-parenting counselor showed me how to sit my feelings to the side and to only deal with the facts of every situation with The Children's Father. Now this was easier said than done. As women, we are naturally emotional creatures, so it was a grave task to not have an emotional response when your character and your parenting is being attacked. Nevertheless, this counselor took a more hands on approach and walked me through how to handle different situations. She showed me how to set a boundary for our communication. Like instead of phone calls and text messages, we'd only communicate via email, so there was a paper trail. But even with that he tried to manipulate the system. He would make obscene accusations in the emails, such as me not allowing him to speak to the girls over the phone or that I was keeping them from him, which was a violation to our agreement. This was a trigger for me, because it was a lie, and I was most afraid that if things escalated with us going back to court that his accusations would be believable. However, I learned that for every attack there is a counterattack. The co-parenting counselor sat and went through replies with me. Replies that only stated facts. Remember, feelings are not facts. There was no spewing off spiteful or hateful remarks attempting to defend myself, but there was however hard evidence to debilitate his lies. If he claimed that he and the girls didn't speak, I would go pull my recent calls and reply with the date, time, and length of the phone call. Having and applying new tactics and a new strategy was my smoking gun.

Now the girls received new strategies in a different way. They struggled most in expressing their thoughts and feelings to their father about whatever made them feel uncomfortable with him and his approach to our new situation. They hated how he negatively spoke about me when they were around and how he would accuse me of brainwashing them because he couldn't accept how they had begun to withdraw from him. So, the co-parenting counselor went through scenarios with them to show them different things that they could do to help them manage during their weeks with him. First it was, "Maybe you can express to him in a respectful way how him saying mean things hurts your feelings or bothers you." Their response, "He's not going to listen. He's just going to say that he's grown, and he can say whatever he wants to say." We had to come to the resolve that whenever he fusses or speaks negatively about Mommy, that they would go into their room to separate themselves from what bothers or upsets them. Then, we had to work through the moments of them not wanting to go back to him on the weeks that he had custody. This was a big one. For a while, when it was time for them to go back to him, they would cry hysterically. This was why he accused me and my family of brainwashing them. He felt that all we did was feed them horrible information or opinions about him as a father and that was far from the truth. The truth was that they hated being around him when all he did was talk bad about me and my family; that's what they shared in counseling. Smoothing out the transitions was a process where they had to come to understand that I couldn't deny him the right to keep them during his weeks. We all had to learn how to adjust. What helped with this was the fact that the co-parenting counselor saw the girls on the weeks with their father as well, so they had something to look forward to. At least they did for as long as he would cooperate. I mean, I wasn't shocked when I found out that after a few months of counseling that he chose to no longer participate. These sessions weren't mandated by a judge, nor was he successful in manipulating the counselor into siding with him about how things should be done, so he bowed out and never completed the program. The girls and I however, absorbed everything we could get.

Both the family and the co-parenting counselor helped my girls and I to make great strides in adjusting. Helped us to accept where we were in life and make the choice about how we wanted to move forward. Though when we started counseling the girls were young, they unfortunately had experienced more than they should have at an early age. They took what was thrown at them and decided to be resilient. As a mom, I pride myself in teaching them to acknowledge their feelings, but at the same time to not allow their circumstances or their feelings to become their crutch. It wasn't going to be the reason that they behaved unseemly or an excuse for them to not progress in school. We utilized therapy as the time to be in our feelings, but when it was time for business and to get our work done, those feelings had to wait.

I remember during my first session with our family counselor, she explained while counseling is great, I should not be in counseling forever. So, with that, we did co-parent counseling for one full year and we did family counseling two to three years. I can confidently say that even today, if I needed our family counselor, her door is still open to us.

The coming out was a long and hard process, but I was willing to do the work, not just for me, but for my children. And we couldn't have done any of it without a support system. Remember that!

Going Through the Process

Nowadays, nobody likes to go through the process, but we fail to realize that there was never a miracle without an affliction, never a breakthrough without bondage or something that you have to go through. Process shapes and molds us for the promise that God has set for our future.

In the midst of my process, there was much pain, much tribulation, much frustration and many, many tears. I know you question, "If you were happily divorced, then shouldn't all of the pain and trauma be done?" I thought so too, but it took someone pointing out how they would see my demeanor change whenever my ex-husband's name was brought up or whenever I was forced to be in his presence. I would immediately get irritated and tense. This made me realize that I was practicing hiding my trauma instead of healing from the trauma. What do I mean? In my mind, I was over allowing him to see how he affected me mentally or emotionally, but on the inside, he was still pressing my buttons. Instead of me focusing on me and what I needed to do to get stronger, I externally spent time trying to convince others and myself that I was okay, while internally suppressing anger, frustration, hurt, disappointment, but most of all fear. You see just because you externally sever the tie with an abuser, doesn't mean that internally or spiritually that tie has been severed as well. That takes a greater work. That deliverance, that stronghold being broken, that soul-tie being severed, didn't come through counseling with my therapist, venting to friends or family, the answer wasn't in a self-help book, and it didn't come through the distraction of being with another man. It came through fast-ing and praying and learning how to love and appreciate ME.

> "For we do not wrestle against flesh and blood, but against principalities, against powers, against the rulers of the darkness of this age, against spiritual hosts of wickedness in heavenly places."

> - Ephesians 6:12 (NLT)

The battle that I was having against demonic spirits showing up in my former husband's behaviors, wanted to take root and rule my mind. Spiritually my emotional and mental capacity was being diminished. Please understand that an idol mind is in fact the devil's workshop. If the enemy can weaken your mind, then the rest of your functionality will follow. I spent so much time obsessing over every threat, the constant character assassination, worrying about the mental and emotional well-being of my children when they were away from me, that I was losing my mind…. LITERALLY! I lived in constant fear and stress over every little thing I THOUGHT was going to happen. The spirit was very intimidating and had such power over my emotions and my thought processes, I even had the thought that it would be better to go back to the man, to grant myself and my children some peace. But thank God I knew better because I know where my peace comes from.

When you get tired of living a certain way, you'll do what you need to do to make a change by any means necessary. Whatever or whoever needs to be cut off, you'll do it. Whatever needs to be readjusted, you'll do it. Whatever sacrifices need to be made; you'll do it. Even if a mental shift is needed and necessary, you'll do it. I knew I had my work cut out for me especially being in such a weak and vulnerable state. The first step had already been made and that was seeking counseling and admitting that I had a problem. Once I began to uncover and understand what my triggers were, and how my ex already knew them and knew exactly how to press them, I could build a strategy. Let me break that down by example. Every mother is sensitive about her children, right? That was DEFINITELY a trigger for me. Well, my children not being with me every single day was my most difficult adjustment. The agreement in the divorce is that the girls are to be able to speak to the other parent every day, but when my ex would get upset, he wouldn't allow the girls and myself to speak to each other. I would call and call and would either get sent to voicemail or wouldn't get an answer at all. Because our specific schedule is from week to week, there were times that I would go days without hearing from or seeing my children. Crazy right!? My initial response was anger. I would lash out emotionally and we had constant conflicts. I was ready to go to all kinds of extremes about my kids, but it took God, the counselor, my wise leaders, and some faithful friends to keep me together. Yes, I made some mistakes in how I handled certain situations, but that's how you learn. One key thing I learned to do to calm down, was go for walks. I would pace up and down the street of my parents' house and I wouldn't stop until God granted me peace and/or direction. This is where I learned that the spirit that was attacking me wanted to argue and fight. He thrived off of it because it allowed him to know that he still had control over me. He took pleasure in making me suffer by not allowing me to have contact with our children, which again was controlling. You have to know that when God grants insight, He will also grant strategy and direction. So, what did I do? I stopped calling and I stopped responding. This was SO hard! I felt like I was abandoning my children in a way. I had thoughts like, "what if they think I don't care to talk to them?" or "what if he feeds them lies about how I'm a horrible mother because I don't call to check on them, and they actually believe it?" Well, that was the sacrifice I had to make. I would go an entire week, while they were with their dad, and I wouldn't call, or I wouldn't speak to them unless he allowed them to call me. What made it easier was God reassuring me that my children love me, and they know who I am and what kind of mother I am, but they also knew why I didn't call. Not because I told them, but because they saw firsthand what I was going through. Understand that enduring the process is never easy, but the place and promise of peace is ALWAYS worth it.

I had to learn a unique way to fight and that was by being silent. Proverbs 12:16 says, "A fool is quick-tempered, but a wise person stays calm when insulted." And my silence spoke volumes. Just like that spirit had studied me, the HOLY SPIRIT in me studied him. It reminded me that he craves my reactions. You see, the enemy had a strategy to make me look like a fool who couldn't control her temper so that those reactions could be used against me legally. Thank God for the Holy Spirit! It took some time, but I had to learn how to be still and be quiet. Something I now live by. If we could learn to shut-up and still ourselves long enough, it'll grant God an opportunity to speak, to move and to fight on our behalf. Sometimes we just do too much! And doing too much, causes us to waste time, hindering what God wants to do. Let me tell you, when I learned this, all kind of blessing started flowing. Things began to progress in my life and work out for my good.

Quite often, he would call the police on me accusing me of abusing my children and when they would come banging down the door at random, all they found was calm, peaceful, and healthy children in a peaceful and loving environment. And no, I didn't call and curse him out, I didn't bash him in front of our kids, and I didn't keep the children from speaking to him. I did him one better. I didn't respond or react at all. I used this weapon of silence, and it confused the enemy. He was so invested in trying to get me to react to his nonsense, that it infuriated him when I didn't. Not to say that his behaviors didn't bother me, because I wouldn't be human if they didn't, I just tried my best not to show it to him. Women can be such emotional creatures that we allow our emotions to drive us not knowing that we often drive ourselves into a wormhole.

I used the energy I had to focus on me and moving forward. When I chose to be still and be quiet, God ordered my steps right into a new car, a promotion, and not just 1 or 2, but three raises on my job in a matter of months. I was winning! I was winning because I had aligned myself with the will of God, because I trusted His word and where He was taking me. By the time we got to mediation to finalize the divorce God had granted me instructions on what to agree to and what to ask for. And at any point in the process where I found myself getting emotional because I didn't agree with something, the Holy Spirit would say to me, "Jocelyn, let it be." When it was all said and done, everything, and when I say everything, I mean EVERYTHING, worked out for my good and there is nothing to this day that we agreed to, that I cannot live with.

CHAPTER FIVE

Raising the Standard

I don't want to mislead anyone in thinking that going through this process was easy at all because surely it was not. There was so much that I had to learn about me and a huge hole I had to climb out of. The first year after my divorce, I spent time readjusting, refocusing and settling into a new way of moving. I also began to take on the weight of being a single mom. Though I had the support of my family, everything concerning my children was my responsibility, so some things had to change. Every responsibility that their father and I once shared, I now had to figure out how to manage. I had to make sure I was available or make necessary arrangements to get them picked up and dropped off to and from school. If that meant getting up earlier and getting home later than, so be it. I was the tutor, the cook, the doctor, the house cleaner, the chauffer, and everyone else. I had a groove, but I was still trying to figure out how to make that mental shift.

I was rebuilding something new from the ground up and along the way, I happened to run into an old friend. The reconnection was a pleasant surprise because this was a friendship that I lost while getting into a relationship with my now ex-husband. It may sound crazy when I say that this connection was welcomed, but at the same time I was extremely apprehensive. Let me explain. I love hard. I have no gray areas. When I'm for you, I'm for you and when I'm not, I'm not. With the trauma that I was still dealing with and still being in a vulnerable space, I wasn't so sure about new connections. However, this wasn't someone new, it was someone I already knew. I was most afraid of inheriting something I heard of called "the hero syndrome." Wikipedia recognizes hero syndrome as a "person seeking heroism or recognition, usually by creating a harmful situation to objects or persons which they can resolve." In a more straightforward term, someone coming to take advantage of your vulnerability for their own gain.

Sidenote: Be mindful of people who try to attach themselves to you during the most vulnerable moments of your life. People may come across as a hero but unfold as the villain. Remember the story of Little Red Riding Hood? Evaluate all new or refurbished relationships with time. Time will tell you what a person's true motives are. Just because it looks good and feels good to you, does not mean that it is good for you .

Now, I didn't want to fall into a mindset of expecting this man to save me or fix me, but it did feel good to have a friend again and now in hindsight I can firmly say that he did become my superman, but not in the way you think.

To go from being isolated from friends and family to now having an open door for both was exciting, however, I did proceed with caution. One of my first traumas that I recognized was that I could never trust that people are truly who they first present themselves to be. You know in the beginning people tend to talk a good game, but then as time passes, the layers begin to peel back, and you begin to question some things. That was where I was with everyone. Though he and I weren't pursuing a relationship and we were and still are truly friends, he didn't get a pass on being tested with time either. And because he was someone from my past, this reconnection was something I had to pray about. I was in the process of rebuilding, so I had to ask God if this connection was approved. I didn't want anyone in my life that didn't belong or wasn't going where I was going because I couldn't afford to go backward. Walking into it was cool, but very surface. I wanted to be careful about divulging too much of my life and recent events because I wasn't sure how much he could handle. (Sidenote: Not everyone can handle your testimony. Some use it as a weapon, and some use it as growing tools. You must be in a place to know the difference.)

As time progressed, the more I began to share my story and my life with him, the more we eventually became the best of friends.

The one place we were able to relate was in co-parenting. I didn't realize until I was in it, that no one in my life was a single parent, so having this first-hand insight and guidance on how to adjust was refreshing. One thing I can say I could appreciate about Best Friend was how brutally honest he was with me. It may have stung from time to time, but it was always truth. I can recall the very first honest advice he gave me. As a mother, it was always my responsibility to make sure that my girls' hair was done. So naturally, this was something that I tried to keep up with even though my kids were only with me every other week. Well, my ex going against this and having other people doing my kids hair was a trigger for me. Oh, I was venting like I had never vented before! And Best Friend responded, "You need to check that and get over it. Whatever he decides to do with those kids while in his custody, is his business and you can't do anything about it. Just like when they're with you he can't control what you decide to do. If you can't handle that then this is going to be really hard for you and you'll always be fighting a losing battle. As long as you know that he isn't causing them any harm, then you shouldn't be concerned." It was in that moment that my attitude changed immediately. I can honestly say that was the mental shift that I needed to push me into properly co-parenting and setting boundaries. So even when I found myself becoming irritated by something The Children's Father would do, I reminded myself of this conversation and it always refocused me. From then I began readjusting the boundaries. So much so, that my ex-husband was no longer my ex-husband, he became "The Children's Father" and that was the only way I referred to him. Him as an ex-husband was put into a box, but we'll put a pin in that for the next chapter.

Best Friend taught me some big lessons. Outside of my family and my therapist of course, he was the first person I was able to let my guard down around. Don't get me wrong it took him some time and effort to knock down some walls, because letting people in WAS NOT, and honestly still isn't an easy feat for me. But the more we conversed about life and our many perspectives it reassured me that everything that my ex said about me was a lie. That I actually was strong enough, smart enough, FREE enough to make some solid decisions.

As a man, my best friend was appalled to hear about some of the things that I had to endure while in my marriage. Most times as women, we give and give and give always feeling like it's never reciprocated. We give to our man, our kids, our jobs, our friends, our family and whomever else needs or wants something and I was hoping that this would be different, and he definitely proved it to be and proved it quickly. Birthday gifts, Mother's Day gifts, Valentine's Day gifts and even Christmas gifts were extremely scarce in my marriage and when Best Friend heard this, he made sure that I always had something for every single holiday and sometimes just because. I remember that conversation like it was yesterday. He said, "As long as I'm a part of your life, you won't ever have to worry about not getting something on any holiday because you're worth that. No woman should go without receiving something on any of those holidays." And to top that, not only did he look out for me, but he helped when help was needed with my kids and my family. When I say he raised the bar, he raised the bar. He spoiled me. I wholeheartedly appreciate that he reminded me of what I deserve as a woman because he didn't owe me nor was he obligated to be there for me. Honestly, I thought after hearing and seeing all of my drama, he would've run, but he has always had my back.

Now don't get me wrong, our friendship has been incomparable, but it hasn't always been perfect. My mother used to think that we always agreed, and I would do anything he asked, but quite the contrary. We definitely have had our share of disagreements, but it was with him that I started noticing what my traumas and triggers specifically were. This could be because he was the closest person to me at the time. Our first disagreement, the moment it started to get intense I felt myself going back to the mindset or space I was in when I would argue with my ex. I know that some can relate, that when you are speaking on something that you are passionate about, your voice levels begin to rise. Now, as crazy as it sounds, he was speaking to me about my importance and my value in his life and his frustration with me was the fact that I didn't see it. Though I heard everything that he said, I missed the message because the passion in his tone, translated as hostility to me. Remember I was in counseling, so I was still trying to learn the difference. That was something that had to immediately be addressed and I was grateful that I could communicate this to him without it being a screaming match. We each actually received what the other was saying. Learning to effectively communicate is one of the biggest lessons that sticks with me. I decided that I no longer wanted to give anyone the right to take me back to that space, and the way I had to do that was to make it clear with my best friend in this moment that there was a certain way that I cannot handle being spoken to. We don't always have to agree, but we have to effectively communicate. When he took what I said and applied it, that meant everything to me. That showed me a level of respect and regard for my feelings that I hadn't experienced in an exceptionally long time. So yes, we disagree, and whether we come to a resolve, or agree to disagree, we never disrespect.

Understanding his role and purpose in my life, took some time. I was in a vulnerable and guarded place, so I took the time to observe how he was presenting himself. It was critical that what I was seeing and getting was genuine. It is important to be mindful of and acknowledge the space you're in and operate (or not) from that space. When in a place of vulnerability, wolves in hero's clothing can be drawn to you. People tend to come out of the woodworks seeking you like prey, if they smell that you need to be saved. They miss, or ignore, the more pertinent truth - you need to heal. Acknowledging the space I was in was pivotal; my awareness made me careful of opening up too soon and of giving too much of myself.

Be honest with yourself and set your standards and your BOUNDARIES. Boundaries are an especially healthy practice and necessity when you're in a life readjustment phase. My boundary became, "actions speak louder than words." And if something didn't add up, or sit well with me, I voiced it.

With Best Friend, what supported the phase I was in was his honesty, his consistency, and his transparency. He was everything that he said he was and if there was ever anything I questioned, he had an answer. Because he showed me that from the start, it helped me to let my guard down. Now don't get me wrong, ever so often I would pray and ask God to show me the purpose and the intent of him being a part of my world. Because let's be honest, over time, the purpose and/or the intent can change, but with him it evolved. Even through the ups and downs of life, our bond only grew stronger. We consistently learn and grow together. We push each other to do and be better in every aspect of our lives.

Over the years, I've been able to share with both my dad and my best friend, on two separate occasions this very statement, "If a man comes into my life and doesn't take care of me the way you do, then I don't want him." As every real daddy should, mine covers me spiritually and naturally. And as every best friend should, mine supports me. And let's not forget that they both spoil me AND my girls. They helped me go from being an insecure woman to standing strong in who I am and what I deserve. They make me feel safe. I am not one of those women who say that I don't need a man because if they weren't needed then God wouldn't have created them. The way these two strong men show up for me is unmatched. So, hero syndrome was evident in my situation, but my superman ended up being a divine connection sent to help teach me and redirect me; and for that I will always be honored to have him in my world because I'm still learning and growing every day.

CHAPTER SIX

Closure

Often, I hear that forgiveness is not for the other person, but forgiveness is for yourself. It's not so that they can be free from the wrong that they did to you, but so that you can be free from being held hostage by the pain that you feel. Every year after my divorce, I tried to work this concept with The Children's Father. I would pray, "Lord purify my heart and help me to let go. Even if he never apologizes, please help me to just let it go." I'm a firm believer that it takes more energy to be angry than it does to just be at peace. I was tired of the constant foolishness. Yes, after 1 year and 2 years and 3 years, I was still fighting for peace. Everything was a battle that now had become a cycle. Every summer we would battle about what school the kids would attend. Every birthday we would argue about what the plan was and why we couldn't celebrate together. And we're not going to even discuss how petty things got around Valentine's Day. It was so bad that in every season I knew what to expect.

By the time we got to 2020, four years of being divorced, I had set up so many walls and boundaries between he and I that it resembled Fort Knox. I had a "you do you, and I'll do me" type of spirit and I was okay with that. At this point I had thrown closure out of the window. Too much damage had been done and too many lies had been told and I was determined to maintain the peace I had gained by any means. Our kids were older, so my parents and I had made a point to purchase them their own cell phones to cut down the communication between he and I. So, with that, I blocked him. I decided to deny him the access to continue to disrespect me, bully me, belittle me and so on and so forth. If there needed to be any communication had, it was going to happen via email.

My focus was maintaining the peace and progressing my life. I had the opportunity to purchase my first home which was such a HUGE accomplishment for me. One of my goals after being divorced was to show my girls that though life had changed, and we went through something that was hard and quite traumatic, that didn't mean that something good wasn't going to come from it. I wanted them to see that life wasn't over just because our family dynamic had changed. After every obstacle I faced head on, closing on my house was one of the best days of my life. The funny thing about this growth moment was that as soon as The Children's Father caught wind of it, his tune started changing.

Mother's Day 2020 I received a voicemail from him. He left a message saying something along the lines of, "Happy Mother's Day. I just wanted you to know that I love you and I'm sorry for everything I've done..." You might think that was nice of him. It was. I was confused. Why? Because this was a drastic change of behavior. I didn't know whether he was being manipulative, or he was being sincere. I remember I let my daddy listen to the message and he said, "Baby girl, test all things with time." My mother laughed and thought it was joke. My best friend questioned why I even listened to the message to begin with. All I know was that it made my head spin, and I wasn't sure why it affected me at all. I was clear that I no longer loved him, wanted him, we weren't even friends, but it was something about this apology that triggered something in me, and I had to sit in it so that I could figure out what that something was.

So, I decided to be still and be quiet so that the Holy Spirit could explain, and it came down to this. Remember in the previous chapter where I told you that he became The Children's Father and was no longer The Ex-Husband? Well, God showed me that I had never dealt with the trauma of him as an ex-husband. I had put that hurt in a box and tucked it away because I felt that I would never get the closure I needed to truly deal with what he had done to me. It was better to forget that the hurt and shame even existed than to continue to fight for a resolve that I felt would never come. But now he had triggered my trauma with this apology. And if you're wondering, no I never responded to him. Didn't ask where it came from, didn't ask why now. I said nothing. I remember a couple of days later, I was having a conversation with my best friend, and he in his own way, followed up with me about the apology I received and was curious as to why it affected me the way that it did. After I explained, he asked me a question that to me seemed so monumental. He asked, "Well best friend, what can we do to help you deal with it so you can get past it, and it doesn't affect you anymore?" That was an answer that I did not have. I had dismissed it for so long, believing that my feelings would never get acknowledged that I honestly wasn't sure how to deal with it. That was something else I needed to go pray about.

As the days past and time was being tested with The Children's Father along with his sincerity, he became more cordial and a lot easier to deal with. I even unblocked him! Of course, he had to earn that, because let's be honest, after all the abusive behavior, lies and foolishness, my respect for him was non-existent. His approach had softened, and he began to show me that he could actually communicate with me without the disrespect. Now, don't get it twisted, my guard was still up, but I honestly wasn't in a place where I was holding a grudge, I wasn't then, nor am I now, the bitter baby mama. I don't receive any child support, nor do I want any child support. All I genuinely care about is my kids being well taken care of by a present father.

Sidenote: Ladies, if you're done with the relationship, be all the way done. Don't be the bitter baby mama, wasting your energy and time trying to make your child's father's life a living hell or trying to drain him dry financially. Do yourself a favor and be honest about where you are mentally and or emotionally. If you're not ready to let it go, then say that, and if you are, then move on toward healing.

For some time after this infamous voicemail, The Children's Father was constantly asking to have a one-on-

one conversation with me. My follow-up was always, "What are we talking about?" and if I couldn't get a clear answer or an answer at all, then we don't need to talk because I always felt like it was a set up. You see, that's what trauma will do to you. It will put you in a place where you don't trust, everything is suspicious, and your guard is ALL THE WAY UP! You see I had vowed to myself that I would never have another sit-down conversation with him ever again because it would always end up being some manipulative tactic or some huge argument. It was more important to me to protect my peace over being caught up in the trap of curiosity that would only lead to a place of setback.

So, one day, while exchanging the girls, he asked yet again for a conversation. I simply replied, "What is it that you would like to talk about?" He took that as me blowing him off, but it was honestly a genuine question. So, I said, "We're here now, what do you want to talk about?" He wanted to know how we could move forward. After four years of being divorced he felt as though there shouldn't be any more animosity between the two of us. Now let's remember that I was speaking to someone who never took accountability or responsibility for anything that HE had done. I was ALWAYS to blame. I felt like I was living the lyrics to the song, "Blame It On Me" written by Chrisette Michelle, *"Blame it on me. Say it's my fault. Say that I left you outside in the cold with a broken heart…"* I sat, and I listened intensely to what he had to say so that I could respond accordingly. And when he was done, I looked up at him and responded, "I know you might think so, but I don't have any issues with you, and I have no problem moving forward. However, there are things that I am not willing to deal with such as your hostility and your disrespect. That aggression triggers my trauma, and I won't and cannot deal with that behavior or accept that approach from anybody. So, if we should ever get back to that place, I will retreat back to my bubble, you will go back to being blocked and communication will go back to the way that it was."

We must understand that closure doesn't mean that you let your guard down, or that you relax your standards. Closure is about growth, moving forward and setting boundaries. Closure did not come for me until lessons were learned about where I went wrong. Closure didn't come until I forgave. Closure didn't come until I took back control over my journey and made a solid decision to let go physically, mentally, and emotionally.

I promise, I will never forget the moment after my response, he looked at me after a short pause and said, "I'm sorry for breaking you." THAT! That moment, those five simple words, rang so loud and resonated in me. For YEARS I waited and for some of those years I pressed for this moment. After years of being humiliated, abused, lied on, my character being attacked, and my parenting being threatened; To finally be at the place of acknowledgment and accountability for what he had done to me as a woman and as his now ex-wife was the closure I felt as though God had finally allowed to come. For the next couple of months, he kept apologizing until I asked him why, "Why do you keep apologizing to me?" He had finally recognized his wrongs and wanted to make them right. Now that was God! This closure brought maturity to the forefront. I don't want you all to think that I didn't hurt or offend him at some points along the way because I know I did. Sometimes intentionally and sometimes unintentionally, but it was my responsibility to get that right, not just for him, but for me as well.

After God allowed this chapter to finally have an ending, it started becoming a lot easier to push forward. Are things perfect? Not by a long shot, but progress is definitely happening. I can honestly say that now not just physically, but mentally and emotionally, I have moved on and I have COMPLETE freedom from the trauma and pain of my past. I no longer allow his presence, his character, his attitude, his hostility, or his decisions to affect my moods or how I choose to live my life. When dealing with him becomes too much, I simply put him on pause. Yes, PAUSE! That means, I have the liberty to say, "No I'm not dealing with this right now. I'll get back to you when I have the mental capacity." Moving forward has been refreshing. I regained self-worth not by validation of a man's existence in my world or by his words, but from learning to become content and comfortable with me. Taking the time to re-build my life gave me more to offer as a woman, as a mother, as a daughter and as a friend. It made me more stable and more accountable to and by myself.

My girls are growing, learning, and going through their own processes. At one point I found myself trying to be the mediator to mend some things between them and their father. From the beginning of our breakup, their dad could not understand the strain on the relationship between he and the girls. Four years post-divorce, the girls were older, and it was time for them to talk. I figured if he and I could move forward, then so could he and the girls. I set up some phone conversations once or twice, whenever I could finesse my way into it. I tried to grant understanding where it was needed on both sides as a parent and as my children's advocate, but I quickly realized that I am not God and that's not for me to do. God still has work that He's doing between my children and their father, and I have to be willing to give room for that work to be done. The story is still unfolding but thank God that we are not where we used to be!

CHAPTER SEVEN

The Conclusion of the Matter

Sometimes we think that resolve comes with the other person changing to fit the idea of how, what or who we think they should be. It is not our job to change people. As a matter of fact, we don't even have the power to change people. That's God's job, and only He can do that. So no, The Children's Father hasn't changed as a person, but he has changed his behavior toward me. Most importantly I have changed, I have evolved, I have grown, and I am better! From the age of 20 to now the journey has been great. There were highs and there were many, many lows, but in order to get to the mountain top, you must first go through the valley. I had to learn a lot about me unfortunately through being broken, but the amazing part is when God allowed me to be broken, I saw what was inside of me. I then asked God to take away the ugly, maintain the good, adjust the flaws, enhance the beauty, and shape and mold me into whatever He wants me to be. I went from a 20-year-old girl who was desperate, insecure, naïve, impressionable, and hard-headed to becoming a grown woman with standards, wisdom, strength, independence, but most of all I am sure of myself and who God has chosen me to be. And in this moment, I can say that I am whole as a woman, but my journey is not yet over. I am single and I am thriving. Not looking for any man to come and complete me because God has already done that but waiting for a KING to come and add to me because there is so much more that God has in store for me. So, I encourage you, don't get stuck in the valley. Don't pick at old wounds so that you never heal, but go through your process, heal, and allow your wounds to become beautiful scars. There is no time limit on your journey of healing. You don't have to rush, just as long as you don't stop moving you will reach your place of peace and happiness. Stay close to God for that is where your strength and your direction will come. Learn every lesson quickly and move forward applying what you have learned. Forgive yourself for every failure and bad decision. Let go of fear because it truly is false evidence appearing real and a tactic of the enemy to keep you bound. Don't fight with hate, bitterness, or animosity, but endure using wisdom, strategy, and love because love conquers all. There is light at the end of every tunnel.

> *"….Weeping may endure for a night, but joy cometh in the morning."*
>
> *- Psalm 30:5 (NLT)*

ABOUT THE AUTHOR

Jocelyn Desiree Ferguson, a psalmist, God lover, disciple, an author, and Kingdom builder. She is the daughter of a pastor and the single mother of two beautiful daughters. She ministers as the Musical Director with her parents, Bishop Windsor and Lady Camille Ferguson, Jr., at Kingdom of God Ministries, International, Coral Springs, Florida. Jocelyn comes with a wealth of discernment and wisdom in walking with God. She is a sought-out psalmist and speaker for workshops, conferences and intimate settings. One of her passions is praise and worship and entering into the presence of God.

Jocelyn is the youngest girl of two children born and raised in South Florida. She is an alumnus of Blanche Ely High School and attended college at Clark University in Atlanta and Broward College in Florida. As a minister and creative spirit, Jocelyn's purpose and assignment in life is to encourage and uplift those that feel less than, rejected, or forgotten about. Jocelyn loves to cook, sit on the beach, binge on good movies, and spend quality time with her family and friends.

Jocelyn enjoys being an active leader on her job as a Confidential Office Manager with the School Board of Broward County.

Jocelyn's passion in life is "inspiring single and divorced women and mothers on their journey to healing and wholeness." Experiencing her journey will offer hope in real life circumstances and help you clarify your moral purpose in life. Her goal is to enlighten you and remind you that your wounds don't have to remain wounds but they can be transformed into beautiful scars and a testimony to change lives.